Upwords

Upwords

A FLIGHT OF POETRY
by
Paul Ray

Sonray Press
publisher

*The quotation used at the bottom of
the Preface of this book was written by
Johann Wolfgang Von Goethe
(1749-1832).*

Copyright 2009 by Paul Ray

All rights reserved.
No part of this book may be reproduced or transmitted
in any form or by any means, electronic or mechanical,
including photocopying, recording, or by any information
storage and retrieval system, without written permission
from the publisher.

For information, contact:
Sonray Press, 1320 Cedar Lane, Charlotte, NC 28226

Printed In the United States of America
Sonray Press First Edition

Cover and layout format by gary hixson

ISBN 978-0-578-03647-2

Dedicated to
Patricia, Alexander, and Margaret
with great love and devotion.

Table of Contents

1	Preface
5	Treat All People Like Angels
7	Please Daddy Tuck Me In
8	The Love Of A Dog
9	Ice Tea Torment
10	Little Dreams
12	A Little Sunshine
13	Only God Can
14	Celebrating Christmas
16	The Arriving Train
17	Who Took Away His Sin
19	Some Love
20	A Problem With The Dryer
21	Add Humor To Your Day
22	Like Dad I Want To Be
24	Doing A Job Well
25	Children Prayers
27	Love The Lord And Love Your Neighbor
29	Tiny Timmy Tiddlehoffer
30	Taking Out The Trash
31	God Has A Cure For That
32	Who Do You Love?
33	The Power Of A Solitary Prayer

[TABLE OF CONTENTS]

34	The Good Night Kiss
35	The Day The Computer Died
36	A Serving Heart
37	The Lost Keys
38	Enjoying Nature On A Swing
39	Why Did He?
40	Oh Hush Now My Baby
41	God Is Good
43	Little Missy Busybody
44	Prayer
46	Grandmother-Angel's Kitchen
47	A Search And Rescue Tale
49	Making Gingerbread Men Cookies
50	Let's All Go Home!
51	Love Could Be
52	Waiting On Pizza
53	O Wife Of Mine
54	The Service Of A Saint
56	A Driving Lesson
57	The Captain Of My Soul
59	Missing A Teddy Bear
60	A Mother Is
62	Plink
64	Reviewing The Year

Preface

Throughout my early childhood, my mother and grandmother would regularly read Bible verses, bedtime stories and poems to me, which captivated me and constantly stirred my imagination. I remember looking forward to getting into my pajamas and jumping into bed to hear them read stories about God, Jesus, Abraham, Noah and Moses. Also, I loved hearing the stories and poems about Aladdin, Odysseus, The Destruction of Sennacherib, The Little Brown Bear, Paul Revere's Ride and Wynken, Blynken and Nod.

Likewise, my father would bless me routinely by playing beautiful music from the baroque and classical periods either on his 'cello, our piano or on the new stereo downstairs. For that reason, the music of Bach, Beethoven, Vivaldi, Mozart and others still stir my emotions to this very day.

Those precious moments have been a cornerstone and catalyst to my spiritual and creative development, and I love my parents very much for that.

I strongly believe that what our world needs more of today is for parents and guardians to sit and read more from the Bible, as well as other great works of literature and poetry, to their children and other family members. Also, I believe that the world needs more parents and guardians to expose their child(ren) to the great music of the masters.

If, just for a little while, they would set aside the computer, television, cell phone and video game on a regular basis and pick up a great book and start reading it to their child(ren), they would witness a miracle over time.

[PREFACE]

It is my opinion that their child(ren) would actually begin to thirst for more of the same great literature and music which, in turn, would inspire them, stir their emotions and creativity, and increase their knowledge and appreciation for, not only God's word, but great works of art as well.

It is my purpose and hope, with this little volume of assorted poetic verse, to be a small part of just such a miracle - to encourage, enrich, entertain, enthuse and ennoble you, the reader, and those to whom you may chose to read.

May God bless you and yours richly.

Paul Ray

"A person should hear a little music, read a little poem and see a fine picture every day in order that worldly cares may not obliterate the sense of the beautiful which God has implanted in the human soul."
JOHANN WOLFGANG VON GOETHE
[1749-1832]

Upwords

Treat All People Like Angels

Treat all people like angels
Be kind to all you meet
No matter where they come from
Lay roses at their feet.

Our love is not selective
To just a chosen few
It's to be given freely
To everyone in view.

Treat all people like angels
Give self to them each day
Make children feel they're special
Spend time with them to play.

Put down the work you're doing
Pick up the servant heart
Be blessed to visit shut-ins
Sit down and let them start.

Treat all people like angels
Look out for the good deed
If homeless folks need something
Be first to meet their need.

Sit next to those who lie there
With little time to live
Pray silently for comfort
That only God can give.

[TREAT PEOPLE ALL LIKE ANGELS]

Treat all people like angels
Especially those with hate
Show Christ to the unloving
To help them change their fate.

Show love to struggling families
Give each red carpet praise
Find ways to bring them closer
To God in coming days.

Treat all people like angels
Show heaven where there's hell
Send cards to those in prison
Bring hope to every cell.

And as you touch each person
With love God has for you
You just might see them changing
Into an angel too.

Please Daddy Tuck Me In

I hate to come home tired from a day of stress and strain
To see my brand new arm chair with a big old jelly stain;
And then I grow more anxious seeing paint drops on the floor
Which trace back to the desk which was not part of the décor.

I can not share the feeling that runs deep inside my brain
To walk and step while barefoot on my son's toy choo-choo train;
And when I read new articles on different types of bass
I find the pictures all cut out for daughter's science class.

I'm angered when my ties are used to hold up blanket tents
I simmer when I notice son tries knocking down the fence;
But then my kids at end of day will yank my heart within
And come to hug and say to me, "Please Daddy tuck me in."

It wasn't but awhile ago when son made mommy shout
He tracked in mud and left it there with trails of mud about;
And then there was the soda drink I placed down near my feet
That daughter knocked all over then and spilled under the seat.

I find inside the shed two bikes, with rims without a spoke
The kids tell me about their bikes, they don't know how they broke;
Then there's the time of candlelight when dinner was first class
When daughter bumped the candles burning table with her glass.

I fumed over the broken pane when sonny threw the ball
I fussed at all the pizza stains on carpet and the wall;
But then my kids at end of day will yank my heart within
And come to hug and say to me, "Please Daddy tuck me in."

The Love Of A Dog

It seems like it was yesterday when Dad brought home our pup
With eyes so big and paws so small and tongue that licked you up;
It loved to run around the house and sleep up on the bed
And loved affection very much and barked when it was fed.

Our pup had bells around its neck that woke us every day
It yipped and yelped to tell us it was morning time to play;
Then Dad would grab his slippers and his robe to puppy's chime
And took the pooch out for a walk for bladder training time.

Our dog was such a loving friend that followed every where
When we got sick or had the blues our dog was always there;
The times we went for picnics and we threw the ball for fun
I'd see our dog so happy just to have the chance to run.

And when we had to take a trip or go for spins to eat
No sooner had we climbed on board than dog was in a seat;
With window down his head was out and taking in the breeze
But now and then he'd pull inside to slobber or to sneeze.

It doesn't seem so long at all that pup matured in breed
With silky coat and larger frame and brightness at light speed;
Our dog grew both in beauty and as treasured friend to all
The years with dog in family were the best as I recall.

I look back at all the moments when our dog licked all my tears
And shared his love to comfort me when troubled with my fears;
I do not know what makes a dog so very good as friends
But all I know is they show love and that's what God intends.

Ice Tea Torment

I was sitting on the hot seat and nobody smiled at me
And a voice said, "You're in trouble 'cause you didn't serve ice tea.
You're supposed to give them ice cubes and you always show some class
And you always serve the ice tea in a double liter glass.
Don't you know how it offends them when you offer tea to drink
And they take a sip of lukewarm then they spit it in the sink!
Now because of your offenses you'll be serving twenty years
You'll be drinking only lukewarm and be sent to bed in tears!"
Oh, I felt so bad and shameful for my leaving out the ice
And I looked up in my sadness and said, "I'm sorry," twice.
Then the voice said, "I'll forgive you if you'll do one thing for me."
And I said I'd do it promptly if the thing would set me free.
Then the voice said, "Give a liter of ice tea to brother Sneed;
Once you've done that come and see me and I'll clear you of your deed."
When I heard the thing he told me then I ran to brew some tea
And I sweetened it so nicely and I chilled it perfectly.
Then I put it in a liter with an ample load of ice
And I gave it to my brother with the hope that he'd be nice
But when brother saw the liter he said, "Why can't I have two!
That was not what you were told and what you were supposed to do
You were given grace and mercy just as long as you did right
But since you did not please me you'll have tears all through the night!"
"Hold on," I spoke out plainly. "Now I've heard that same thing twice."
Then my brother said, "I did it so you wouldn't forget the ice."
At that I took the glass from him and poured it on his head
And I went back home to sleep that night and not a tear was shed.

Little Dreams

It's while I'm sleeping in my bed
That little dreams run through my head
I don't know why they change so fast
But all I know is they don't last.
Some dreams with action are intense
Some dreams are strange and don't make sense
Some dreams of mine can get complex
There's no telling what may come next.

I dreamt I once served on the moon
With Special Forces Space Platoon
We were there to guard the craters
From some giant space invaders
In a stealth mode we walked about
But all at once I heard a shout
A giant monster came in view
I fired and "bang" I'm in Peru.

There with my donkeys at my side
I'm carrying gold strapped high and wide
I walk on mountain tops so steep
From treasures found in Inca's keep
Then suddenly a dart hits me
It's poison tipped most certainly
I grab my vile of antidote
I take a sip and start to float.

[LITTLE DREAMS]

    I'm flying in a dirigible
    Along the shores of Istanbul
    A passenger throws me a box
    I hear at once its ticks and tocks
    I leap with bomb as I dispatch
    And toss it down the escape hatch
    The captain steers the vessel wide
    And with the blast I'm ocean side.

    I'm sitting on a windy shore
    While scooping sand I find a door
    I dig it out and turn the knob
    But as I do I hear a sob
    And "poof" a woman's hugging me
    For freedom from captivity
    The lovely genie grants a wish
    Who kisses me and with a swish -

    I'm laying in my bed again
    Not sure she heard my wish, but then
    I look outside and there I see
    A shiny new red Ferrari.
    I jump up and dash for a ride
    And see a note with keys inside
    I start it up, the dashboard gleams
    The note attached says, "In Your Dreams."

A Little Sunshine

Give a little sunshine
Erase away a fear
Bring a little extra joy
To someone needing cheer.

Do an act of kindness
To wish is just a crime
Show a little courtesy
By giving of your time.

Embrace and kiss your loved ones
Share love and tell them why
Tomorrow is not promised
Don't let the day go by.

Put others first before you
Live just to make their day
Remembering Christ's example
To serve and love and pray.

Only God Can

My child I see you hurting there and wish to ease your pain
And know that I am just someone who cares;
I wish that I could turn time back so you could start again
Then you could not reflect on hurtful errs.

The only one that heals the heart is watching down on you
And knows your agony and inward grief;
God is the great physician and his words are always true
Trust in him and hold tight to your belief.

I pray for you each day and night that God will heal your heart
For he is holding you in loving arms;
There's nothing that's impossible that he can so impart
For this is part of God's own secret charms.

The Lord is coming back again to take us all away
And you my child are standing first in line;
The heaven gates will open as I hear the Master say
Come home my child and now forever shine.

Celebrating Christmas

It's such a wondrous season
To share our love and sing
And have a birthday party
For Christ our heavenly King.

Though malls are always crowded
With people running wild
Remember what's important;
The gift of the Christ child.

While in the crowds be Jesus
Give gifts to everyone
It's love and hope we offer
And reason for God's son.

Bless others while you're waiting
In lines and parking lots
Show Christ in acts of kindness
By giving up your spots.

Rejoice in God forever
Give praises as you pray
Keep celebrating Jesus' birth
Have Christmas every day.

While sharing gifts with others
Be sure they feel the love
Let others see the love in you
Which comes from God above.

[CELEBRATING CHRISTMAS]

    The Christmas lights are lovely
    And candles burn so bright
    But nothing shines like Jesus
    The babe who brought the light.

    The meals we have with family
    Are times we all hold dear
    So share your life, the gift from God
    With laughter, love and cheer.

The Arriving Train

I hear the whistle blow for the four forty five
And see the people gather to their feet;
The railway signals flash as the bells come alive
As parents nudge their children from their seat.

Conductor stands his ground and warns all to stand back
The music of the station starts to rise;
A steaming sound is made, as train sounds click and clack
And waving cries are heard with tearful eyes.

The train comes to stop with a final blast of steam
Conductors start to exit with some cases;
Crowds begin to chatter and children run and scream
To greet their family members with embraces.

Oh isn't this a picture of how it will be
When we all get to heaven by and by;
We'll be at home forever with God's family
And the sweetest music there will never die.

Who Took Away His Sin

He needs the Lord so bad
I know his heart is hurting
His eyes are red from tears
From reckless words he's blurting.

He does not realize
The mess that he is in
If he could just remember
Who took away his sin.

He moans while he's asleep
And yells with sudden cussing
He bangs around in bed
And rolls while he is fussing.

I'm not so sure he knows
That drink will do him in
If he could just remember
Who took away his sin.

He's loud and has no friends
And yells, "Who ya lookin' at?"
The people quick their steps
As they run away from that.

I'm sure if he got dry
And started over again
Then he could soon remember
Who took away his sin.

[WHO TOOK AWAY HIS SIN]

    I'm going to be his friend
    And be gentle as a dove
    I'll tell him of the Christ who
    Transcends anger into love.

    It's through the love of Christ
    That hope and joy begin
    To repent and be baptized
    And take away his sin.

    And now he goes out sharing
    God's love he's now a part
    He reads to folks each day
    From the book that changed his heart.

    If God saved a sinner
    Like the one above was in
    Christ can sure help save you too
    And take away your sin.

Some Love

Some love the sound of the bubble wrap
Some love what's found from a treasure map
Some love the flight of a hummingbird
Some love insight by a well-placed word
Some love the fact cowboys move the herds
Some love to act without wasting words
Some love the smell of hot apple pie
Some love to dwell on the reasons why
Some love the wind blowing through the trees
Some love to end war and offer peace
Some love to place all their sights dead on
Some love to face all their fears head on
Some love the sight of a sunset sky
Some love to fight where our freedoms lie
Some love the cream on banana cream
Some love to dream an amazing dream
Some love the nights on the open sea
Some love the lights on a Christmas tree
Some love to teach where no one will try
Some love to reach where the starving die
Some love is giving up life or limb
Some love is living for God in him
One love is free if we hear his call
One love is He who has died for all.

A Problem With The Dryer

I remember of a day that I was cleaning house;
The chores had been put off. Don't ask me why.
I was doing laundry then to help my dear sweet spouse;
With piles of dirty clothes to wash and dry.

Clothes were in big stacks that I did not want getting higher;
And sheets were stacked up in a separate pile.
Grabbing up some hot damp clothes I tossed them in the dryer;
They'd be completely dry in just a while.

I had left the clothes to dry while spinning round and round,
And walked away to mop the kitchen floor;
Suddenly I heard a shriek with hissing in its sound,
"Bang, bang!" as something hit the dryer door.

I had jumped a foot or two and ran back with a shout,
And quickly looked inside the dryer bin.
I could not believe my eyes as kitty flopped on out,
And laughed to see the state that she was in.

My poor kitty walked around with hair fuzzed up and blown;
I told her that I knew that she was mad.
She was sleeping in a clump of clothes that I had thrown,
And looked at me with eyes that looked so sad.

I held kitty in my arms and rubbed her little head;
She purred at once to tell me all was well.
I then gave her food to eat but she chose drink instead;
The water was refreshing, I could tell.

So from now on when I wash and when I dry the clothes,
I will look around the piles just to see.
For I do not want the dryer frying kitty's nose,
And do not want one more catastrophe.

Add Humor To Your Day

If your life has lost its laughter
If your weeks are without wit;
If your days drum up depression
Then tell jokes to humor it.

Since our lives are quickly fleeting
As the time ticks youth away;
We should practice playing pun games
And add humor to our day.

It is stress and strife that shorten
All our days to some degree;
So to cure our disposition
We should add some comedy.

It's so sad when some are somber
Living in their solemn ways;
We should try to lift their spirits
And bring laughter to their days.

God gives all the gift of humor
So laugh long while being kind;
And be playful, pure and peaceful
Have a happy frame of mind.

So the next time tension tightens
While your head just pounds away;
Just scoop up a cup of cheerful
And add humor to your day.

Like Dad I Want To Be

I used to think my dad was strict
When I had to do my chores;
As soon as I got home from school
I was told to sweep the floors.

I did not understand back then
That my dad was training me;
To learn to work and not to shirk
My responsibility.

I still remember of the day
I stepped on a hornet's nest;
He grabbed me up and shielded me
To avoid the stings, I guess.

Another day a Scottie pup
Whimpered at me, looking lost;
He knew how much I wanted one
So he helped me pay the cost.

A giving heart,
A serving heart,
A loving heart has he.
Except for Christ, a life's pursuit;
Like Dad I want to be.

[LIKE DAD I WANT TO BE]

There was a time my throat was sore
When my tonsils were removed;
My dad had brought me sweet ice cream
And praise God, how much it soothed!

There were some days I felt so bad
When I wish I had stayed in bed;
But then he came and cheered me up
We had movie time instead.

The Bible that he gave me in
December of seventy-nine;
Has been the gift I love the best
And I treasure it all the time.

And each Christmas is a highlight
Of the way he shows his love;
His gifts of sacrifice are great
Which are all sent from above.

A giving heart,
A serving heart,
A loving heart has he.
Except for Christ, a life's pursuit;
Like Dad I want to be.

Doing A Job Well

How many times have you heard it's been said,
"When doing a job do it well?"
The trouble with that is we all make mistakes
And most times we try we will fail.

To start a pursuit takes tenacity so
Have patience to grow with insight
But most of all time is the thing we must have
To learn 'til it's finally done right.

Failures are teachers we must grow to live with
If ever we want to succeed
Learn not to fear them and learn how to cheer them
While budding in wisdom and deed.

Beware all the insults and pressures you'll get
From those who will not support you
Don't listen to them and stay focused on task
And progress will work it's way through.

Musicians aren't born playing all perfect notes
And scholars must earn each degree
Language is something not learned overnight
And neither is Christianity.

So stick to your call and work hard at your task
And always present just your best
For if you do that you'll know job is well done
Since God will help fill in the rest.

Children Prayers

When some little children pray
They'll bow and close their eyes
They'll pray that they'll be strong and brave
And God will make them wise.

They pray to the Lord to bless
Their loving Mom and Dad
And always ask the Lord for help
In good times and in bad.

Their words are so soft and sweet
With little hands they fold
They have a heart that's full of love
And faith that's purest gold.

The angels of God will hear
And fall down on their knees
And praise the Lord of Heaven above
For prayers from such as these.

And as little children pray
They ask forgiveness too
And ask that God will help them with
The things they ought to do.

And even in prayers sometimes
They'll pray for cats and dogs
Their hearts reach out to all their pets
Including fish and frogs.

[CHILDREN PRAYERS]

> God loves innocence like this
> He wants more hearts like these
> The prayers of little children that
> Bring angels to their knees.
>
> If only adults could pray
> As children do so well
> By pouring hearts out to the Lord
> The praise to God would swell.

Love The Lord And Love Your Neighbor

Someone was a little child
Who scattered sunbeams when he smiled.
He loved to hug and kiss a lot
And most say never cried or fought.
The words of wisdom that he spoke
Amazed the old and wiser folk.
I'm sure if they asked his advice
He'd say without him thinking twice,
"Love the Lord your God with all your heart
And love your neighbor as a start."

Someone was a teenage boy
Who brought his mother constant joy.
He worked and helped his dad with care
To build and sell each desk and chair.
He loved to go to church and teach
How far and high God's love will reach.
If someone asked which law was best
I'm sure he'd speak and pass the test,
"Love the Lord your God with all your heart
And love your neighbor as a start."

Someone was a lonely man
Who showed love like no other can.
He healed the sick and raised the dead
Fed hungry souls with grains of bread.
But then a friend accepted fees
And gave him to authorities.
Through trial and torture words were few
Yet still he showed the truth he knew,
"Love the Lord your God with all your heart
And love your neighbor as a start."

[LOVE THE LORD AND LOVE YOUR NEIGHBOR]

Someone died upon a tree
And shed his blood for you and me.
His body buried for three days
Then raised again for all to praise.
He said that he will come again
To take us home who're free from sin.
So follow him at any price
And follow his own great advice,
"Love the Lord your God with all your heart
And love your neighbor as a start."

Tiny Timmy Tiddlehoffer

Tiny Timmy Tiddlehoffer
Was a mean and hurtful scoffer
Who would tease and act malicious
And would mock and be so vicious.
But despite his disposition
Tim did right with his position
Helping orphans as a token
Since his home was torn and broken.

Tim was always in detention
For the words that he would mention
Making children cry with sadness
And the teachers shriek with madness.
When he left the seat he filled in
He would help some orphan children
With their reading and their writing
Learning Dickens while reciting.

Tim would spend his extra hours
Bringing waifs more books and flowers
Teaching them to learn addition,
Gardening, cooking and nutrition.
But one day he read some verses
That he got from in-school nurses
Which he loved with great affection
And caused him to change direction.

Timmy came apologizing
To the school as he stood rising
Telling all his sins confessing
Knowing now God's son and blessing.
From then on Tim grew in kindness
Filled with love which cleared his blindness
He was still quite small by measure
But to God he was a treasure.

Taking Out The Trash

I heard the dump truck down the street -
"Get out there with the trash!"
These words my father yelled as I
Ran outside in a dash.

I flung the trash cans to the curb
With all the bags in tow
And heard the trash man yell at me,
"'Bout time" and "Way to go."

My father told me after that,
"Do not procrastinate.
For if you do it frequently
Your troubles will inflate."

"Remember son," he said to me,
"A job's worth doing well.
Don't wait, don't rush, just be like ants
And not like bats from hell."

I thanked him for his point and said
That things wouldn't be the same
For trash cans now would be in place
Before the trash men came.

I worked each week from then on out
As diligent as ants
To get the garbage problem solved
Since I was given the chance.

I learned a lesson early on -
The wisdom not to wait;
To get rid of all trash within
Before it was too late.

God Has A Cure For That

Are you feeling down?
Don't know where to turn?
Have a constant frown?
Face is always stern?

Do you have no peace?
Feeling all alone?
Anger will not cease?
Heart is cold as stone?

God has a cure for that.

Is your life a mess?
Don't know what to do?
Is your answer yes?
Haven't got a clue?

Stumbling in the dark?
Frozen from the fear?
Can't get out of park?
Engine not in gear?

God has a cure for that.

Hear a pleading sound?
Feel a painful heart?
Need to turn around?
Would you like to start?

Hear the savior's call?
Want to live again?
Will you give your all…
Living free from sin?

God has a cure for that.

Who Do You Love?

I had a dream and a voice said to me,
"Who do you love without hesitancy?
Do you love serving the lost and the poor -
Giving to bless them then giving some more?
Do you sit hearing them tell of their pain,
Then you encourage again and again?

If not the poor, could the sick be your call -
Listening and wiping each tear that may fall?
Do you love holding their hands close in yours
And share with them God's love which endlessly pours?
Do you read stories to brighten their day
And do you give hugs and throw kisses their way?

If not the sick, could the old be your love -
Who you hold dearly and always think of?
Do you love hearing them tell of their past -
Learning of lessons from life passing fast?
Do you give honor where honor is due
And praise them for sharing such wisdom with you?

If not the old, could the rich be your passion -
Trying to fit in and imitate fashion?
Do you waste time with your hunger and greed -
Striving for wealth which is empty indeed?
Do you think people with money and stuff
Can be content and say, 'I have enough?'

If not the rich, with pursuits full of dross
May I encourage you follow the cross.
There you'll find someone who died there for you -
Who rose to give life to all followers true.
He loves the poor, sick, old, rich, all above -
The question is yours now, 'Who do you love?'"

The Power Of A Solitary Prayer

A soul drifts
Tearful eyes closing in anguish
Bitterness permeating a hurting heart
Revenge echoing in a judgmental mind
Idle hands preparing for an attack
Rage ignited to the point of imminent detonation
Feet readying to run for the cause of hatred
The viper of distrust is about to strike
The hornet of prejudice is about to sting
Self is quickly invading the entire body
The plague of the I is growing and infecting the spirit
Screams of eternal torment and death are an earshot away
The body leaps aimlessly into action and then ...

From a distance words reverberate from an earnest prayer,
"Please God let Jesus change his heart!"

The body is thrown suddenly face down on the ground
There is an immediate silence to these spoken words
A snapshot of a cross flashes brightly in the back of his mind
There is the projection of a solitary bloody figure hanging in torment
The figure raises his head and looks directly at him crying out
"I love you but why do you crucify me again?!"
The heart immediately shoots with pain from the dagger and convulses
The rage quickly turns to peace
The mind begins to recite over and over again requests of forgiveness
The heart begins to beat again to love
The eyes begin to water again in gratitude
The hands begin to fold again to pray
And the feet begin to run again to serve
Hallelujah! Self has been destroyed!
Praise be to God that the I has been crucified and buried!

What a difference a solitary prayer can have on a soul.

The Good Night Kiss

Little eyes look at you as you kiss their head good night
They look at you intently as you're turning out the light
Little lips will ask you for a hug before you go
You come and hold them in your arms because you love them so
Little hands will hold you while the lips say, "I love you"
Your eyes begin to tear up as you tell them you do too
Little ears have heard at last the words that they've longed to hear
They know that all is well again and nothing's there to fear
Little lips will tell you then they want to be like you
You tell them that you're proud of them for everything they do
You comfort them with words of love while giving them their bear
You let them know that God is love and knows their every care
Little hands let go of you and feel the bear's soft touch
You rise again and tell them that you love them very much
You tuck them in their covers in a blanket of moon beams
You slowly close the door at last and wish them pleasant dreams.

The Day The Computer Died

There was a day I won't forget my hard drive died on me
The processor gave up the ghost and lost its memory;
I just sat down to start some work with soda drink in hand
I turned it on, I heard a buzz, and when it popped I ran.

Electric burning smelly smoke filled up the room so fast
I had to turn the fans on quick to blow away the gas;
And after that I yanked the plugs to minimize the loss
But still I knew my CPU was nothing now but dross.

I pulled the flash drive from the port and checked it carefully
To see if it was damaged since it held my poetry;
I plugged it in my laptop which I kept in closet stored
And finding all my work was saved I cried out, "Thank the Lord!"

I went with daughter to the store to buy another one
And had a father-daughter time with both just having fun;
We walked along computer aisles and saw a lot of things
We shared some games, we heard some songs and played with cell phone rings.

We finally found the CPU which had great bang for buck
But when the salesman came to us he said, "You're out of luck.
That model has been all sold out. There's nothing we can do."
We thanked him, turned to leave, but no; the owner came in view.

He came to me at once and said, "Oh yes, we'll make your day.
We'll let you have a better one; cost difference we will pay."
My daughter picked a good one with some extra gigabytes
At home we swapped the old with new and then turned on its lights.

So now I've learned a lesson here I did not see before
It's in the midst of tragedy God blesses so much more;
I now know why I could not save the hard drive by the cord
God gave me precious gifts of time with daughter, Praise the Lord!

A Serving Heart

I thank God for your Christian love
For giving me your best;
Your selfless acts are from above
Which sacrificed your rest.

I cannot think what drives you to
Put other things aside;
Except that you have Christ in you
And self's been crucified.

When times are tough as prices soar
You volunteer to give;
There is no doubt you've found the Lord
And know whose life you live.

And when the sun sets in the sky
Death knocking at your door;
Then God will say you'll never die.
Rejoice forevermore!

The Lost Keys

It was not too long ago that I saw things get out of hand,
When my kids had practice in karate and in marching band.
They had just told me to hurry so that we would not be late;
So I rushed to eat my sandwich and rinsed off my dinner plate.

I had gone to get my wallet on the dresser in my room,
While I heard the sound of teenage children yelling doom and gloom.
As I went to grab my wallet which I always placed with care;
It was then I leapt in panic when I saw my keys weren't there.

I went looking on my dresser then I looked down on the floor,
Then I looked behind the table and around the closet door.
When I did not see my keys around while down upon my knees,
I then shouted to my children, "Please help Daddy find his keys!"

Soon the sounds of children running could be heard throughout the place,
As they rushed like little banshees with some anguish on their face.
I heard clamor in the kitchen as they all began to wail,
And I heard a shriek of silence as they stepped on kitty's tail.

It was kitty's howl that shocked me into thinking of the past,
As I started to remember when I used my car keys last.
I had used my keys that morning getting groceries from the store
And while I put up the groceries I placed them... inside a drawer!

I went running to the kitchen and pulled out a drawer with ease,
And looked down inside the sliding box and saw my set of keys.
While I shouted, "Hallelujah!," my two kids came back in view,
And they told me both together, "Let's get going!" And we flew.

Oh the things we have to go through when we're put into a bind;
They could all be settled quickly letting God just clear our mind.
So the next time you're in trouble when you can't find your car keys,
Do not wait for kitty's shrieking; have a quick prayer on your knees.

Enjoying Nature On A Swing

I sat enjoying peace one night reclining on my swing
And watched the clouds unfold the moon while hearing tree frogs sing;
The wind blew gently through the leaves which made their rustling sound
While scents of roses filled the air and fireflies flickered 'round.

As stars were shining overhead like diamonds all aglow
I sat there staring up to watch God's great nocturnal show;
The moon was full as it could be and brightened up the sky
Then played a game of hide and seek as all the clouds went by.

Just then I heard a barred owl hoot which came out of the blue
It seemed to only want to know "the cook who cooks for you;"
And to this song the crickets chirped out in the field next door
Who kept the tempo with the owl like they've done that before.

I heard the gentle gurgling sound of water in a brook
That flowed nearby and shimmered bright when last I took a look;
And not far off a rabbit stood to see what was ahead
But when the owl called out again, the hare dropped down and fled.

Two deer came out in distant field and stood in moon's bright light
They grazed awhile then walked away, like ghosts into the night;
Some geese flew past in standard form and honked as they went by
As if to say that night was here and just the time to fly.

I loved to feel the gentle air flow all around my face
As I would swing both back and forth in that enchanted place;
It feels so good sometimes for me to get away from things
And watch in quiet solitude to see the gifts God brings.

Why Did He?

Why did he love when no one loved him back?
Why did he walk when soldiers would attack?
Why did he see while bleeding from his eyes?
Why did he trust when all he heard were lies?
Why did he think with thorns inside his head?
Why did he smile while friends all turned and fled?
Why did he stand while pain throbbed from his hips?
Why did he scorn the myrrh brought to his lips?
Why did he speak while heaving for each breath?
Why did he pray while at the brink of death?
Why did he save a sinful dying crook?
Why did he give a final loving look?
Why did he hang from a cross in that place?
Why did he cry when his God turned his face?
Why did he ask that God forgive their sin?
Why did he call to take his spirit in?
Why did he keep your soul from Hades' fire?
Why did he come to save his soul's desire?
Why did he die like that to set men free?
Because he is the God of love you see.

Oh Hush Now My Baby

Oh hush now my baby and start into dreaming
The day has expired and the stars fill the sky
Your room is filled up with the moon's brilliant beaming
And angels have come to protect you and I.

From out in the field I hear crickets sing after
The sound of a coo from a sweet morning dove
They sing every night and live life full of laughter
Because they have peace from the master above.

Oh rest now my precious and know God is present
The maker of all of the seas and the lands
He loves every person, both noble and peasant
And holds all the cares of the world in His hands.

When sleep comes eternal I pray you'll be singing
In glory in splendor in honor and praise
I pray in His arms you'll be holding and clinging
And be filled with laughter for infinite days.

God Is Good

God is so good
Grab his hand and you'll see
He has dreams just for you
He has dreams just for me.

He wants you to give
All your life just for him
And live every day
Loving out on a limb.

God is so great
He's the creator of all
He formed all the heavens
And all creatures that crawl.

He sees when you sin
And knows all your pain
He has given you Jesus
To cleanse every stain.

God's word is active
For it reads every heart
If you follow his word
Watch a miracle start.

God is the love
That no words can express
God's spirit brings comfort
By his simple caress.

[GOD IS GOOD]

God is the master
There's not a thing he can't do
So ask God for help
So he can start to help you.

Hold on to God
Don't let go! Never fear!
God is good, God is great
God is love and God is here!

Little Missy Busybody

Little Missy Busybody
Comes to wish you well
Wants to hear a juicy secret
So she'll go and tell
Doesn't matter where it comes from
Just so long it's good
She just wants to get acceptance
As she thinks she should.

Little Missy Busybody
Loves to chatter on
Talks about the sins of others
Even though it's wrong
And if she's confronted by it
She'll make quick reply,
"I don't mean to harm," she says to
Cover up her lie.

Little Missy Busybody
Doesn't really care
She just wants to see the shock from
Rumors that she'll share.
She will seek a chance for leverage
When she needs it most
For a price she'll keep her silence
This she loves to boast.

Little Missy Busybody
Don't stir up God's wrath
Know that gossip will destroy you
If you stay this path
God is always there to hear you
If you will repent
And does love and will accept you
Through his son he sent.

Prayer

The way we draw our strength from God,
Is prayer;
A time when we are blessed and awed,
Is prayer.
When we try hard to give all men,
The love of Christ that we are in;
A place where we should all begin,
Is prayer.

If someone has a hurt, the need
Is prayer;
The way for us to plant a seed
Is prayer.
Though life will bring its twists and turns,
As we have heartaches and concerns;
The only way to heal what burns,
Is prayer.

The greatest way to stop a doubt
Is prayer;
What also cleans us inside out
Is prayer.
If we're not sure what we should say
But want to give God's love away;
The best gift we can give today,
Is prayer.

A way we praise the Lord above,
Is prayer;
The life line to eternal love
Is prayer.
If there's a sin we should confess,
An act caused by our selfishness;
The place where God will clean our mess,
Is prayer.

[PRAYER]

A quiet time down on our knees,
Is prayer;
A time with food and families,
Is prayer.
Let's read and share good news today,
It's Christ who washed our sins away;
The way to start and end each day,
Is prayer.

Grandmother-Angel's Kitchen

Oh, the love in her kitchen, I treasure it still
With the vase of blue cobalt that sat on the sill
I woke every morning to a sizzling pan
And I sprang out of bed - to the kitchen I ran
I grabbed her and hugged her and thanked her for lovin'
And thanked her for cooking the treats in her oven
The joy in her kitchen all come back to me
Oh, the sounds, and the smells, and the love - Heavenly!

Oh those biscuits she made were so awfully good
While in Grandmother-Angel's white kitchen we stood
Our mouths were all drooling from all of the smells
And we froze there in awe as if under her spells
Then my granddad would chuckle while carving the ham
And mother just smiled as she brought out the jam
The joy in her kitchen all come back to me
Oh, the sounds, and the smells, and the love - Heavenly!

From the door I saw cardinals that sat in the pine
And heard doves that all cooed from a telephone line
As I did Granddad opened an old cookie tin
And he offered us cookies and treats from within
Then I heard her say loudly to put them away,
"It's time to get seated, to hold hands and pray."
The joy in her kitchen all come back to me
Oh, the sounds, and the smells, and the love - Heavenly!

We would sit at the table and Dad would give grace
And I felt the sweet stillness of love fill the place
Through the sound of the tick of the clock on the wall
And the sound of our collie who played with her ball
What a beautiful blessing to share in his love
With Grandmother-Angel who came from above
The joy in her kitchen all come back to me
Oh, the sounds, and the smells, and the love - Heavenly!

A Search And Rescue Tale

When I walked along the river
I saw tracks you left behind
There were signs of blood on branches
And the fear grew in my mind.

As I called for you to answer
I heard movements faint ahead
Running hard I searched and found you
Laying still and almost dead.

Then I screamed your name in anguish
Seeing that your gash was great
I tore my shirt to make a bandage
Praying I was not too late.

Throwing scarf and coat around you
Shielding you from frigid wind
Yelling loud that someone help me
I carried you my faithful friend.

In my car I laid and held you
Driving fast with head in arm
Praying, asking God would save you
As I thought what caused you harm.

Medics took you in quite quickly
I then sat with eyes closed tight
Praying, hoping for God's mercy
Pleading life with all my might.

[A SEARCH AND RESCUE TALE]

Feeling then someone had touched me
I looked up and saw a smile
Hearing then that you'd recover
But you'd have to rest awhile.

A year's gone by my loving fellow
Your health's back, no longer frail
I love your kisses and affection
But most of all your wagging tail.

Making Gingerbread Men Cookies

Shortening, sugar, syrup dark and sweet
Flour, baking soda and some milk
To make a treat.

Nutmeg, ginger, cloves and cinnamon
Thrown into a mixing bowl
And stirred and stirred again.

Oh the smell of gingerbread
Cookies in the air
Children standing by the trays
Waiting for them there.

Dough cooled, then rolled on a cutting board
Little men are all cut out
Then baked and cooled and stored.

Gum drops, icing, little ginger men -
Cookies have been all dressed up so
Eating can begin.

Oh the smell of gingerbread
Cookies in the air
Children gobble up them fast
None are left to spare.

Let's All Go Home!

See a chance to serve another
Don't look down, go help your brother
Move your feet, put them in action
There's no greater satisfaction
Than to know you've been like Jesus
That's the way we hope God sees us
Loving, serving, giving the day
To the Lord, no time to delay.
Let's all go home!

While the day may have it's troubles
Share the love until it bubbles
Overflowing on another
Giving hope but not to smother
Sharing all the news of Jesus
'Til the day he comes and frees us
From this world that we are dwelling
To a home of glory yelling
Let's all go home!

This life's short and quickly fleeting
Know God's heart and hear it beating
As you share your life with brothers
Die to self and live for others
Make the most of every minute
Thanking God for sharing in it
Looking to the celebration
When we're part of that great nation.
Let's all go home!

Love Could Be

Love could be a little boy
Who saw a neighbor cry;
He went to hold her in his arms
And stayed 'til tears ran dry.

Love could be a little girl
Who went to nursing homes;
She hugged and kissed most everyone
And read them books and poems.

Love could be some strangers who
Gave to a charity
Instead of being recognized
They gave anonymously.

Love could be a homeless man
Who got cash on the street;
But when he saw another starve
He bought them food to eat.

Love could be a teenager
Who planned a trip abroad
But when her family church burned down
She gave the cash to God.

Love could be a neighbor who
Came to a family's side
She brought them food both day and night
Because a child had died.

Love could be so many things
But love is never free
God's greatest picture of pure love
Is Christ at Calvary.

Waiting On Pizza

We waited for the pizza to
Arrive by six o' three
But when an hour past that came
I sensed hostility.
"What's taking it so long to come!"
My daughter cried and said,
"It's only two large pizzas with
A side of garlic bread."

I called the store to find out why
Our pizzas had not come
But when I asked, the lady laughed
And started acting dumb.
"Why John came back an hour ago.
The pizzas have been sent."
I told her then no pizzas came
And kids were getting bent.

At that she said, "Excuse me please,"
And then she left the phone.
I waited as I overheard
Her speak and then a groan.
With that she got back on the line
As sweet as she could be,
"I'm sorry sir you had to wait.
The pizzas will be free."

I thanked her as we disconnected
And told my kids the news.
They jumped with joy as wailing stopped
And gave no more boo hoos.
The pizza was delivered then
To feed my family.
We finally got free pizzas at
The time of eight o' three.

O Wife Of Mine

O wife of mine, O wife of mine, your heart is just adored by me!
When day is done and I come home, your love is always poured on me.
With kisses stored for me,
And not ignored by me.
Whatever hurts or cares I have, you love to come and share with me -
You come and share with me
Because you care for me.

O wife of mine, O wife of mine, oh blessed angel sent to me!
I'm lost without your guiding hand and loving spirit lent to me.
Your love is meant for me,
And time is spent for me.
I feel my heart keep turning round as your love keeps on molding me -
You keep on molding me
With your hands holding me.

O wife of mine, O wife of mine, please know that I am here for you!
I hold you close within my heart and I will always cheer for you.
Through every year with you,
And every tear with you.
You have a strength found in the Lord that I know is not rare for you -
It is not rare for you
For Christ is there in you.

O wife of mine, O wife of mine, God's smiling in the skies at you!
You touch the hearts of souls each day denying self that lies in you.
Christ has a prize for you,
And sees God's eyes in you.
I know a host of angels sing their songs of joy above for you -
They sing above for you.
I give my love to you.

The Service Of A Saint

How can we who know the gospels
Sit back with our lips all sealed?
Didn't Christ and the apostles
Call us all to work His field?

Should we not all serve each other
As we're thanking God above?
Do we give a future brother
Sacrificial gifts of love?

So let's strive to turn the battle
Fighting hard to win all souls;
Moving hearts until they rattle
And at times by heaping coals.

Christ has warned us of the trouble
That we'll face while in his fold;
We must sift through people's rubble
To help change their lives to gold.

We should always trust in Jesus
As we walk the extra mile,
And believe the one who sees us
May know Christ in just awhile.

We must teach about salvation
As we share from God's own word;
Some will need to know creation
And the way that sin occurred.

[THE SERVICE OF A SAINT]

If we ever want the spreading
Of the gospel shared abroad,
We should start at home by getting
On our knees and pray to God.

Then with courage and devotion
We'll share Jesus on our street,
And be Christ in constant motion
With each person that we meet.

A Driving Lesson

Just like in an action movie
Watching daughter drive the 'UV
Making heart beat hard and faster
Waiting for a great disaster
Swerving past a dark Mercedes
Nearly clipping two old ladies
Screaming, yelling, "please slow down!"
Then she does but with a frown.

Peeling past the supermarket
People seem to be her target
Dodging every car she passes
Daughter steers to miss their chassis
Jumping back in anger yelling
Some words children ask the spelling,
"Look out now, don't drive so fast!"
So she does and takes the sass.

As the light is changing yellow
Daughter speeds and then I bellow,
"Slow your speed and start your braking,
If you don't, the keys I'm taking!"
Then at once she drops her speeding
Knowing privilege is fleeting
For the driving times with Dad -
So she stops but she is sad.

Then I thought of my first lesson
Driving as my dad was stressin'
Helping me to drive while learning
As his knuckles too were turning
White from fear and the commotion
But I saw his great devotion.
Then I told the child of mine,
"Sweetie, you are doing fine."

The Captain Of My Soul

While in the final moments
Of this momentary realm
I'll see the ship of freedom
With my Savior at the helm.

The glory of the Lord will shine
Through sails of gleaming white
And penetrate the angel wings
That stand in clouds of light.

I'll share my parting words of love
With family and with friends
Then tell them Christ has come for me
To sail where life begins.

Oh come to me my Captain
And the master of my soul
Sail home with me to paradise
As clouds and thunder roll.

Brief were the toils of hardship
With their worry, stress and pain
But when at last I sail back home
I'll have no strife again.

I'll have a home forever
With the Lord and saints abroad
All joy and love will glorify
The majesty of God.

[THE CAPTAIN OF MY SOUL]

    The flagship of the Savior
    Always sails to heaven's shore
    And carries souls who give their lives
    To Christ forevermore.

    Oh come to me my Captain
    And the savior of my soul
    You gave me passage on your ship
    Because you paid the toll.

Missing A Teddy Bear

Once there was a teddy bear who fell behind a bed
It fell into a hidden spot when Sally moved her head;
She was traveling with her dad back home to Monterey
And thought her bear was in the seat of Daddy's Chevrolet.

Sally loved her bear a lot and took it everywhere
While propped up to her booster seat she always held it there;
But this time the bear was left in guest room twenty-three
At Motel Six on Fitzgerald in downtown Pinole.

Many miles on down the road is when she finally spied
Her precious bear was missing so she pouted and she cried,
"Teddy bear is missing. I don't see him next to me.
Please Daddy stop and find my bear. Oh where, oh where is he?"

Sally's daddy stopped the car and looked but could not find
The teddy bear which Sally loved and gave her peace of mind;
Then while looking all around she gave another yell,
"I think I left my teddy bear back at the last motel!"

Sally's dad then smiled and said, "I'll call. That's what I'll do.
I'm sure if bear is in the room they'll send him back to you."
Kissing Sally on the cheek he drove without a sound
And called the Motel Six that night to see if bear was found.

Three nights passed without the bear next to her tiny side
And every night the bear was gone the little girl just cried;
Then a box with teddy bear came home that lit her face
It was a day that Sally saw a gift of loving grace.

A Mother Is

A mother is a brilliant star
Who shines light night and day
She teaches children how to act
And shows them what to say.

She has a heart that's full of love
And spirit full of joy
She always tries to brighten up
Her little girl and boy.

A mother is intuitive
And sacrifices time
She comforts and she counsels and
Does not hold back a dime.

She looks for good in everything
And does not think of self
She is a great physician when
A child of hers needs health.

A mother is forgiving when
No other will forgive
And loves her children faithfully
As long as she does live.

She will not let a chance slip by
To hold and kiss a face
And treasures all the moments when
Her child seeks her embrace.

[A MOTHER IS]

When failures come and troubles knock
A mother hopes and prays
Her children will endure the storms
To grow in coming days.

But most of all a mother is
A gift from God above
Who is a light to every child
And shows God's precious love.

Plink

Lying in my bed one night
While I was counting sheep;
I heard a constant dripping sound
That woke me from my sleep.

I rose from bed and walked into
The bathroom to the sink;
Because I thought the faucet leaked
With its annoying "plink."

I tightened handles with my hands
And then went back to bed;
Assuming that the leak was stopped,
I laid my weary head.

But, as the sheep were lining up
For counting in my brain,
I heard a sound go "plink, plink, plink"
Start right back up again.

I bolted up and ran back to
The bathroom sink once more,
And twisted tight each faucet knob
Then closed the bathroom door.

I jumped in bed with pillow clutched
Around my ears and head,
Still came the sound of "plink, plink, plink,"
And not the flock instead.

[PLINK]

When finally I could not withstand
The dripping sounds I heard,
I got up like a crazy man
And screamed, "This is absurd!'

Then standing by the sink again,
I listened for the "plink,"
And as I stood, I heard the sound,
But from the tub, not sink.

I bent and turned those handles tight
And then went to my room;
Embarrassed that I blamed the sink
For my nocturnal gloom.

And soon I started counting sheep,
As one more time I tried;
But not a sheep went "baa, baa, baa,"
T'was "plink, plink, plink," they cried.

Reviewing The Year

I like to look back through the year
And see as best I can;
The service, both for good and bad
I gave my fellow man.

I always start by thanking God
For giving me his son;
To start each day and end each day
In praise for what he's done.

And moving then on down the line
I note all of the good;
Then plan next year to do the same
As this is understood.

And then I try to figure out
Of what I can improve;
So when I face that thing again
I hope it will run smooth.

Each thing I see that needs more work
I try my best to change;
But only through the grace of God
My life can rearrange.

And then at last I try to see
What new things I can do;
To bless each one the coming year
So they'll bless others too.

The poems in this book were set in 10 point
Century Schoolbook.

OTHER POETRY BY PAUL RAY

If you enjoyed

Upwords
A FLIGHT OF POETRY

you may also like

Scattered Glimpses
LEAVES OF POETRY
ISBN 978-0-578-03646-5
available online at lulu.com

www.ingramcontent.com/pod-product-compliance
Lightning Source LLC
LaVergne TN
LVHW091318080426
835510LV00007B/547